# Causes of the Civil War

of the

by Susan Buckley

# TABLE OF CONTENTS

**INTRODUCTION**

**The First Shots of War**

When cannon fire exploded across Charleston harbor on April 12, 1861, the United States had come to the end of the road to war. It would take four years and more than 620,000 lives to reunite the nation.

**CHAPTER 1**

**Growing Up, Growing Apart**

As the United States developed, how and why did the Northern and Southern regions of the nation differ?

**CHAPTER 2**

**Slavery: At the Heart of the Conflict**

What role did slavery play in the conflict between the North and South?

**CHAPTER 3**

**The Firebell in the Night**

How did the United States try to resolve the conflicts over slavery and states' rights?

**CHAPTER 4**

**The Road to War Is Paved**

What were the final events that led to the Civil War?

**CONCLUSION**

# THE FIRST SHOTS OF WAR

At 4:30 on the morning of April 12, 1861, cannon fire exploded. It blazed across the harbor in Charleston, South Carolina. The bombing of Fort Sumter had begun. Shells hit the forty-foot-high walls. This early-morning attack would start the bloodiest war in American history. The war would rip the nation apart. What led to the attack that spring morning? What caused this very long and violent conflict?

▲ The bombing of Fort Sumter lasted more than thirty hours. By the following day, it was clear that war had begun.

The soldiers who fired were Americans. So were the soldiers in the fort. A few months earlier, these men were fellow countrymen. They were all citizens of the United States of America. Then in December 1860, the state of South Carolina voted to secede, or leave the United States. Six other Southern states soon followed. They left because Abraham Lincoln had been elected president. The Southern states joined together to form the Confederate States of America. The thirty-three American states were now two nations.

Lincoln took office. His goal was to keep the Union together. The country wondered how he would do that.

Fort Sumter presented a major problem for Lincoln. The fort would soon run out of supplies. If Lincoln sent a supply ship, Confederate soldiers might fire on it. That would start the Civil War. If Lincoln did not send supplies, the fort's commander, Major Anderson, would have to surrender to the Confederates.

The Confederacy also faced a problem. If the Confederates fired on the fort, they would be starting the Civil War. They were not sure they could win a war. Nevertheless, they decided to fire on the fort. They were fighting for their way of life. As Confederate Robert Toombs said, "The firing upon that fort will inaugurate a civil war greater than any the world has yet seen."

The shots fired on Fort Sumter ended any hopes of reuniting the country. The Civil War had begun. What had led the United States to this moment?

▲ Major Anderson surrendered Fort Sumter on April 13, 1861. A Confederate flag flew over Fort Sumter until the end of the Civil War in 1865.

# GROWING UP, GROWING APART

As the United States developed, how and why did the Northern and Southern regions of the nation differ?

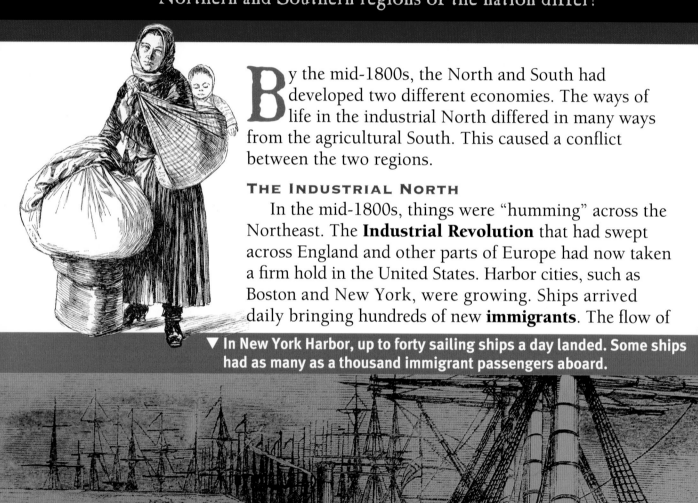

By the mid-1800s, the North and South had developed two different economies. The ways of life in the industrial North differed in many ways from the agricultural South. This caused a conflict between the two regions.

### THE INDUSTRIAL NORTH

In the mid-1800s, things were "humming" across the Northeast. The **Industrial Revolution** that had swept across England and other parts of Europe had now taken a firm hold in the United States. Harbor cities, such as Boston and New York, were growing. Ships arrived daily bringing hundreds of new **immigrants**. The flow of

▼ In New York Harbor, up to forty sailing ships a day landed. Some ships had as many as a thousand immigrant passengers aboard.

people to America had been going on for centuries, but it became a flood in the mid-1800s. Between 1845 and 1855 alone, three million immigrants crossed the Atlantic to the United States. The Northeast was their first stop.

People were leaving the farms to move to towns and cities. There they found work in factories. In Lowell, Massachusetts, waterwheels turned machines in forty cotton **mills**. Inside the mills, more than 10,000 workers tended the large machines. Many were women and children. In 1850, there was more industry in Lowell than anywhere else in the nation. The mills of Lowell produced about one million yards of cloth every week!

▼ The factory system in New England towns like Lowell was new in the 1800s.

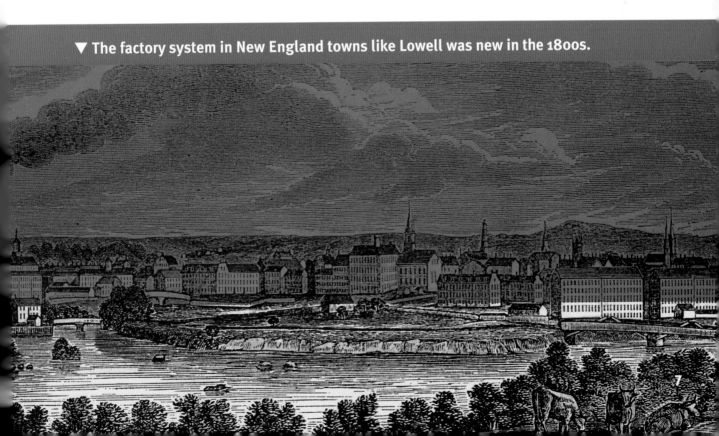

Progress was also being made in transportation. Workers were building canals, roads, and railroads across the Northeast. Many of these workers were immigrants. In New York, the Erie Canal opened up the shipment of goods between the Midwest and the Northeast. Steamships crossed the Atlantic, carrying goods and passengers. By 1850, the United States had more miles of railroad track than any country in the world, and many more miles of track were soon to be built.

New means of communication, such as the telegraph and newspapers, were also developed during this time. New technology and inventions, such as the lightweight steel plow and the threshing machine, improved farming. The United States was becoming highly industrialized. Most of this progress was taking place in the Northern states.

▲ Many of the builders of the Erie Canal were immigrants.

▼ The inventions of the Industrial Revolution sped up progress in the New World.

▲ In the 1850s, trains like this one were transforming travel and shipping. This train took three days to carry 360 people and the U.S. mail between New England and the Midwest. In the past, it would have taken sixty wagons three or four weeks to make the trip.

▲ Samuel Morse invented the telegraph in 1837 and changed communication forever. Messages that had once taken days or weeks to be delivered now arrived in seconds.

▲ Inventions like the grain thresher and Eli Whitney's cotton gin increased the rate of food and textile production.

# CHECKPOINT ☑ READ MORE ABOUT IT

The mid-1800s were an age of invention. Many of these inventions changed how people lived. Read more about important inventions, such as the telegraph, the sewing machine, and the mechanical reaper. Tell how these changed people's lives.

## THEY MADE A DIFFERENCE

A "Yankee" invention—the cotton gin—transformed the cotton industry. Connecticut-born Eli Whitney invented the gin in 1793. It allowed workers to clean up to fifty pounds of cotton a day and increased the Southern production of cotton a thousand times from 1830 to 1860. The cotton gin transformed the South from a mostly tobacco- and rice-based economy to a cotton-based economy.

### THE AGRICULTURAL SOUTH

A visitor to the South would have seen a world very different than the North. Farms—from small farms to huge **plantations**—covered the land. While the North had many industries, the South depended on farming. Even in big cities, such as New Orleans and Charleston, businesses centered on farm products, such as tobacco and rice. However, one crop came to dominate all the others.

Cotton became the South's most important crop. People called it "King Cotton." Growing cotton was at the center of Southern agriculture. By the mid-1800s, three-quarters of all the cotton in the world came from the American South. Much of it went to Great Britain's textile mills. Southern cotton also supplied Northern mills, such as the ones in Lowell.

Southerners needed cheap labor to grow cotton profitably. **Slavery** provided that cheap labor. So, the massive production of cotton in Europe and the Northern United States depended on the labor of millions of enslaved African Americans in the South.

| Percentage of Slave Population to Total Population Southern States, 1790–1860 | | | |
|---|---|---|---|
| Year | Southern States | Border States | Lower South |
| 1790 | 33.5 | 32.0 | 41.1 |
| 1800 | 32.7 | 30.8 | 40.3 |
| 1810 | 33.4 | 30.1 | 44.7 |
| 1820 | 34.0 | 29.6 | 45.6 |
| 1830 | 34.0 | 29.0 | 46.0 |
| 1840 | 34.0 | 26.7 | |
| 46.0 | | | |
| 1850 | 33.3 | 24.7 | 45.4 |
| 1860 | 32.3 | 22.3 | 44.8 |

# Cotton became the South's most important crop. People called it "King Cotton."

▲ Enslaved people worked from sunup to sundown picking cotton.

Most white families in the South owned no slaves. However, on large plantations, hundreds of enslaved men, women, and children worked the fields. They labored to produce King Cotton. The slave population grew rapidly. About one-third of all Southerners were African American by the mid-1800s.

In the North, about a quarter of the people lived in cities. But in the South, most people lived in **rural** areas. Unlike the waves of immigrants moving into Northern cities, few immigrants settled in the South.

It was slavery that made the North and the South so different. As a writer in the *Charleston Mercury* newspaper said in 1858, "On the subject of slavery, the North and South . . . are not only two Peoples but they are rival, hostile Peoples."

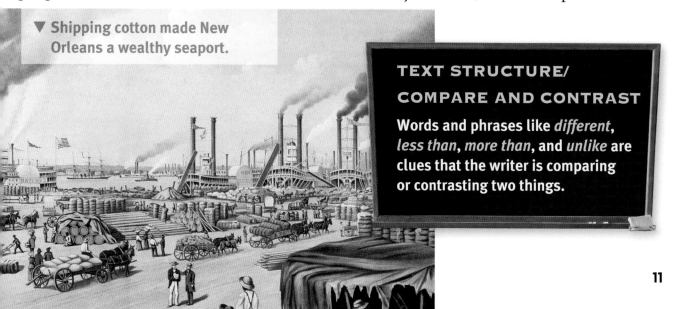

▼ Shipping cotton made New Orleans a wealthy seaport.

## TEXT STRUCTURE/ COMPARE AND CONTRAST

Words and phrases like *different*, *less than*, *more than*, and *unlike* are clues that the writer is comparing or contrasting two things.

## THE WEST

In 1852, Marian Russell left Kansas with her family in a covered wagon. She was seven years old. They were traveling west on the Santa Fe Trail. For Marian, it was an exciting adventure as "sturdy pioneers blazed trails across a strange and wonderful land of prairies, plains, and mountains."

**Pioneers**, like Russell and her family, were people who were moving west to unsettled lands. These people were moving to the huge area west of the Mississippi River that stretched all the way to the Pacific Ocean. They were seeking new land to farm.

The settlers built farms and then towns and cities. In time, they wanted their new territories to become states. They wanted to join the United States. But new states posed a difficult problem. Some settlers to new territories had brought their slaves with them. They wanted to join the United States as states that allowed slavery. Other settlers formed new territories without slavery. Would the new territories become **slave states** or **free states**? This question became a problem for the American people. Over time, it led to the Civil War.

▼ Like these pioneers on the Oregon Trail, Americans moved west for new land and new lives. America's population had grown dramatically, from 4 million to 23 million between 1790 and 1850. By 1860, over half of all Americans lived west of the Appalachian Mountains.

## SLAVE OR FREE?

By the 1820s, slavery had been abolished north of Delaware. In January 1850, the United States consisted of thirty states. In fifteen of them, slavery was allowed. These were known as "slave states." In the other fifteen, slavery had been abolished. These were known as "free states."

# SUMMING UP

- By 1850, the United States was a large and wealthy nation with widely differing regions.
- The North was in a period of growth and progress. Great changes in industry and transportation were taking place. Immigrants from Europe were swelling the population.
- The South, on the other hand, remained mainly agricultural. Its economy, based largely on cotton, was made possible by slave labor.
- As the nation expanded west, the problem of slavery made the differences between the regions greater.
- As new states joined the United States, the critical question was whether the state would be admitted as a free or a slave state.

# PUTTING IT ALL TOGETHER

Choose one of the activities below. Work independently, in pairs, or in small groups. Share your presentation with your class.

**1** If you lived in a small New England village, would you have gone to work in the mills at Lowell? Why or why not? Search online to learn more about the lives of mill workers of Lowell. Then write a diary entry from the point of view of a "Lowell Girl," describing a day in your life in Lowell.

**2** Research Eli Whitney and the cotton gin. Work with a partner to present opinions of the cotton gin by a plantation owner and an enslaved African American. Debate how the invention changed lives.

**3** Create a map of the United States in 1860. Be sure to label all states and territories. Include a key that shows the major jobs and resources for each region.

# SLAVERY:
## At the Heart of the Conflict

What role did slavery play in the conflict between the North and South?

Slavery played an important role in the colonies right from the beginning. A group of English settlers arrived in Virginia in 1607. They founded the colony of Jamestown. Just ten years later, the first Africans arrived. They worked in the tobacco fields. By the late 1600s, most Africans brought to America were enslaved.

In 1776, Thomas Jefferson wrote in the Declaration of Independence that "all men are created equal" and have a right to "life, liberty, and the pursuit of happiness." Yet enslaved African Americans were not treated as equal to whites and were not free.

▲ The Africans brought to Jamestown worked with the English colonists. Historians believe that these first Africans were servants, not slaves.

## PRIMARY SOURCE

"Representatives . . . shall be apportioned . . . according to their respective numbers which shall be determined by adding to the whole number of free persons, including those bound to service for a term of years, and excluding Indians not taxed, three-fifths of all other persons."

From the Constitution of the United States, Article 1. The Legislative Branch

Slavery soon became the center of bitter fights among the men who created the U.S. Constitution. They had to decide how many representatives each state would have in the government. They based this number on how many people lived in a state. But how would slaves be counted? The South wanted to count each slave, while the North did not want to count them at all. Finally, Congress passed a law that said slave owners could count each person they "owned" as three-fifths of a person.

**THE ROOT OF THE MEANING:**
In American history, the word

# ANTEBELLUM

refers to the period before the Civil War. It is made up of two Latin words: *ante*, meaning "before," and *bellum*, meaning "war."

### THE PLANTATION SYSTEM

Through the first half of the 1800s, cotton production and slavery grew together. The invention of the cotton gin made producing cotton far easier and more profitable. But cotton production in the **antebellum** South depended on slave labor. As cotton production increased, so did the number of slaves who produced it.

### SLAVE LIFE

▼ When some people picture the antebellum South, they see huge white homes, pillared porches, women in hoopskirts, and men on horseback. The reality was very different from this romantic picture. Most white Southerners did not live on plantations. Life for the African Americans who lived there was far from romantic.

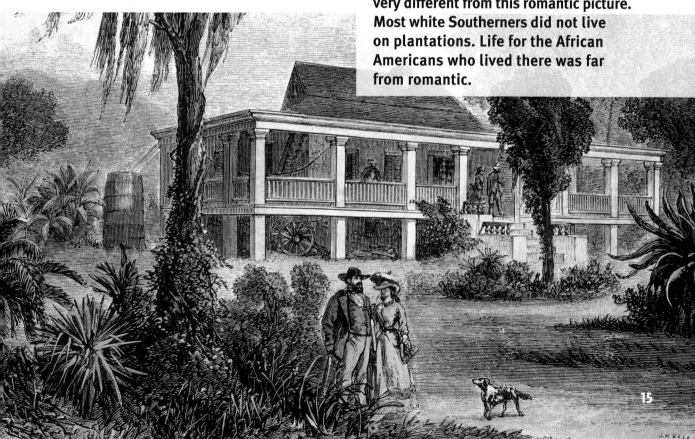

Life for most enslaved African Americans was harsh. They worked from sunrise to sunset. During harvest time, they worked eighteen-hour shifts. Men, women, and children worked in the fields or as house servants. Many lived in simple huts on the plantations, sleeping on straw beds. They had few clothes. Food was basic, perhaps cornbread, greens, fish, and rarely chicken or pork.

The worst part of slavery, however, was that people were treated as property. They could be bought, sold, or inherited. Families could be broken up, separating parents and children. Slave codes forbade slaves to read or write, meet with free African Americans, or leave plantations without permission.

As difficult as life was, African Americans managed to hold on to many of their African traditions. They told stories orally, passing on their history to their children. They also passed on dances and songs from Africa. They grew food they knew from Africa, such as yams and rice. Family ties were also greatly valued, as they had been in Africa.

## HISTORICAL PERSPECTIVES

The Southerners who grew cotton needed slaves. So, many defended slavery. In 1837, South Carolina senator John C. Calhoun said this in defense of slavery: ". . . let me not be understood as admitting, even by implication, that the existing relations between the two races in the slaveholding States is an evil:—far otherwise; I hold it to be a good, as it has thus far proved itself to be to both . . . Never before has the black race of Central Africa, from the dawn of history to the present day, attained a condition so civilized and so improved not only physically, but morally and intellectually."

## RESISTANCE, REVOLTS, AND A "RAILROAD"

Enslaved African Americans wanted to be free, but escape was almost impossible. Slaves were valuable property. Overseers watched slaves' every move. White Southerners passed laws that required slaves to carry written "passes" in order to move about. Slave owners used bloodhounds to track runaway slaves. Slaves caught escaping were whipped, or lashed, hundreds of times. Those who did escape, often had trouble finding food or shelter on their journey North.

Still, enslaved people found ways to resist. Some pretended to be sick or organized "work slowdowns" in the fields. Some destroyed crops and tools. Others resisted by learning to read and write, or by carrying on African traditions forbidden by their owners.

What white slave owners feared most were revolts, or rebellions. On some occasions, enslaved people did rebel. Nat Turner led the most famous rebellion in 1831 in Virginia.

## PRIMARY SOURCES

Today we can learn the true story of slavery from people who lived it. Historians have collected letters that slaves wrote or dictated. Once free, people like Frederick Douglass and Harriet Jacobs wrote memoirs about their lives. Former slaves were interviewed about their experiences. These slave narratives help us "see" slave life.

In 1834, former slave James R. Bradley wrote this in a letter. Bradley had bought his own freedom.

"I have said a good deal about my desire for liberty. How strange it is that any body should believe that a human being could be a slave and feel contented

... I know very well that slaveholders take a great deal of pain to make the people of free states believe that this class [is] happy and contented—and I know too that I never knew a slave—no matter how well he was treated—that did not long to be free."

# CHECKPOINT ☑ READ MORE ABOUT IT

Imagine that you are an enslaved African American. How would you resist or work against slave owners? Read more about how slaves fought against slavery.

"I never knew a slave—no matter how well he was treated—
# that did not long to be free."
—James R. Bradley

On August 21, Turner and a group of followers killed more than fifty white people. They brutally killed men, women, and children. Turner and most of his men were soon captured. Turner was tried and hanged. Then whites took revenge. Southern whites murdered more than 200 African Americans in cold blood. Harsher slave code laws were passed. These laws were used to control the actions of free and enslaved African Americans.

▼ Levi Coffin, an Indiana Quaker, helped thousands of African Americans escape from slavery. In this scene, he and his family welcome a group of fugitives on a winter morning. He ignored the risks and worked to help the escapees.

▲ Harriet Tubman was perhaps the most famous of all the conductors. Tubman fled slavery in Maryland in 1849. She led hundreds to freedom. People called her Moses.

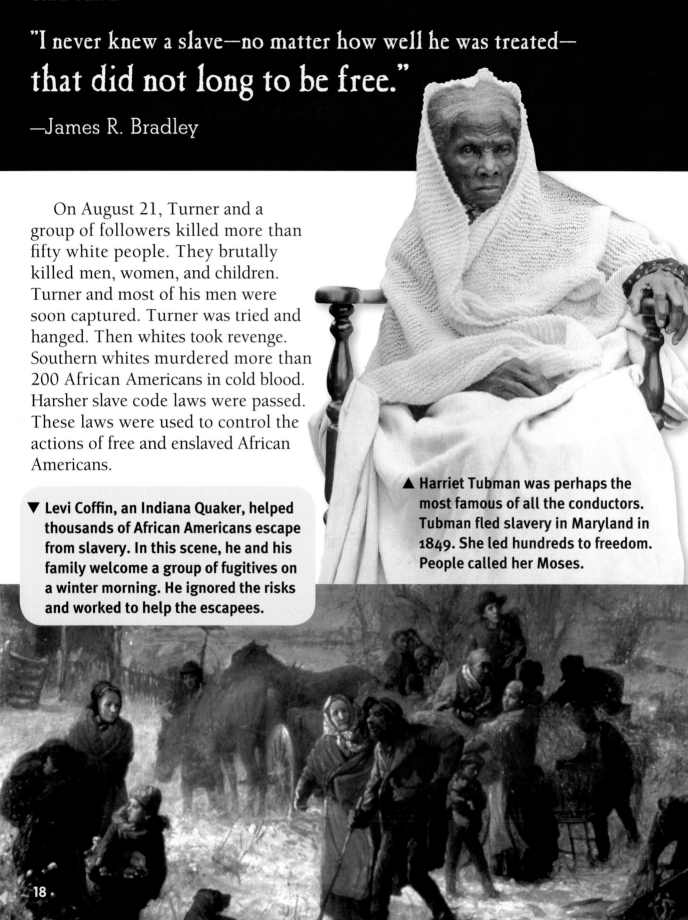

▲ Light-skinned Ellen Craft pretended to travel as a white man with her husband, William, as her "slave."

▲ William Still is called the "Father of the Underground Railroad." He was an active conductor who helped up to sixty people a month escape from slavery through Philadelphia. He also published more than 600 escapees' stories in a book called *The Underground Rail Road*.

Nat Turner's failed revolt did not stop slaves from escaping. Beginning in the early 1800s, slaves began to escape from the South via a remarkable network. It came to be known as the **Underground Railroad**. It was neither underground nor a railroad. It was a system of "conductors" who guided escaping slaves to "safe houses." Hiding by day and moving by night, the slaves traveled North to freedom. Everyone involved took great risks. For aiding an escaping slave, fines were $1,000 and six months of jail time.

## ABOLITION AND ABOLITIONISTS

## THEY MADE A DIFFERENCE

Henry "Box" Brown was a slave in Virginia. He escaped by mailing himself in a box to abolitionists in Philadelphia. Later, he became a speaker against slavery and a showman.

# THE LIBERATOR

"I will be as harsh as truth, and as uncompromising as justice . . . I am in earnest—I will not . . . excuse—I will not retreat a single inch—AND I WILL BE HEARD!" With these strong words, William Lloyd Garrison started a newspaper in Boston. It was called *The Liberator*. His paper would become the voice of the **abolitionist** movement.

Abolitionists were people who worked to abolish, or end, slavery. They had been active since colonial times. But in the years before the Civil War, their cry to end slavery grew louder. Their goals were both to **emancipate**, or free, the enslaved and to help **fugitive** slaves escape.

Two years before *The Liberator* appeared, African American David Walker published his *Appeal*. In this pamphlet, he urged slaves to rise up and rebel. He told white Americans to end slavery "for your own good." Some people believed that Nat Turner's rebellion took place because of the urgings of Walker and Garrison.

As the movement heated up, women began speaking out in public for the first time. Before this, "proper" women did not speak in public. These women were not afraid of breaking convention. They wanted their voices to be heard. So African American women like Maria Stewart, Sojourner Truth, and Harriet Tubman made public speeches against slavery. So did white women like the Grimké sisters. In 1838, 3,000 women—both black and white—met in Philadelphia at the Anti-Slavery Convention of American Women.

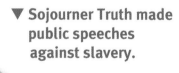

▼ Sojourner Truth made public speeches against slavery.

# The Liberator became the voice of the abolitionist movement.

An angry mob gathered outside. When the women left the meeting, they were stoned. The following day, the mob burned down the building. Changes were in the air. Some thought the changes were dangerous.

That same year, a young man escaped from slavery in Maryland. He was Frederick Douglass. Douglass would become a great American leader. Within a few years, his accounts of slavery would become a powerful call for abolition.

## ☞ HISTORICAL NOTE

Abolitionists published this song about Frederick Douglass. The "peculiar institution" was another name for slavery. The song sheet ironically calls Douglass "a graduate from the peculiar institution."

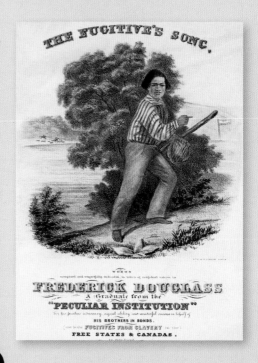

## THEY MADE A DIFFERENCE

Sarah and Angelina Grimké were unusual abolitionists. They grew up on a South Carolina plantation, the daughters of slave owners. Rejecting slavery, they spoke out with the power of those who had seen it firsthand. "I stand before you as a Southerner, exiled from the land of my birth by the sound of the lash and the piteous cry of the slave. I stand before you as a repentant slaveholder," Angelina said when she spoke to the Massachusetts legislature in 1838.

**Sarah Grimké**

**Angelina Grimké**

▲ A proslavery mob in Illinois shot and killed Elijah Lovejoy, who had printed antislavery articles. The American Anti-Slavery Society declared "Lovejoy the first martyr to American Liberty, Murdered for asserting Freedom of the Press." The mob depicted here destroys Lovejoy's printing press.

## ABOLITION BACKLASH

Not all people who lived in the free states in the North were abolitionists. Some did not agree with them. Over time, many abolitionists became more extreme in their views and actions. So some people tried to stop them. An angry mob chased William Lloyd Garrison through the streets of Boston, trying to hang him.

People in the South fought against the abolitionists. They passed laws to tighten their control over African Americans. Southern states made it illegal to teach black Americans—free or enslaved—how to read and write. They passed laws that limited freedom of speech and the press. In Tennessee, a mob whipped a minister for handing out antislavery materials. A mob invaded a South Carolina post office to destroy bags of abolitionist mail.

People all over the country were discussing the issue of slavery. No matter which side they were on, people were passionate about their opinions. The issue of slavery became a key part of every political debate.

### TEXT STRUCTURE/ CAUSE AND EFFECT

Phrases like *as a result* and *because of* are signals that the writer is making a cause-and-effect relationship.

# SUMMING UP

- Slavery was at the center of the conflict between Americans in the first half of the 1800s.

- Southern plantation owners defended the institution of slavery. They came to depend on slave labor more and more as cotton became their major crop.

- Other Americans—both black and white— worked to end slavery.

- Not everyone agreed with the abolitionists, some of whom developed extreme views.

- For enslaved African Americans, the challenge was to survive and to maintain their individuality and their culture.

# PUTTING IT ALL TOGETHER

Choose one of the activities below. Work independently, in pairs, or in small groups. Share your presentation with your class.

**1** Create a diorama of a plantation. Label its different parts, such as fields, slave quarters, and the main house.

**2** Research what happened to the slave trade. When was it ended and what were the effects? Then write a "newspaper article" on the subject.

**3** Research Harriet Tubman. Then reenact a journey on the Underground Railroad, led by Tubman.

# THE FIREBELL
## IN THE NIGHT

How did the United States try to resolve the conflicts
over slavery and states' rights?

Slavery had been a problem for a long time. It troubled Jefferson
when he wrote the Declaration of Independence. As time passed,
the issue of slavery became even more troublesome. The delicate
balance between the number of slave states and the number of free
states continued to change. In 1819, members of Congress debated
whether Missouri should be admitted to the Union as a slave or free
state. Jefferson was long out of government by that time, but he
followed the debate with concern. The debate led to the Missouri
Compromise (see page 27), which was passed in 1820.

▲ Kentucky senator Henry Clay played a central role in the congressional
debates over slavery. In his efforts to keep the Union together, Clay
became known as "the great compromiser." He led the drive to work
out both the Missouri Compromise and the Compromise of 1850.

The decision, "like a firebell in the night, awakened and filled me with terror. I considered it at once as the knell [death] of the Union."

—Thomas Jefferson on the Missouri Compromise

Jefferson was alarmed about the Missouri Compromise. He believed that it was dangerous for Congress to pass laws about slavery. The decision, "like a firebell in the night, awakened and filled me with terror. I considered it at once as the knell [death] of the Union." He believed slavery should be left alone to die out on its own.

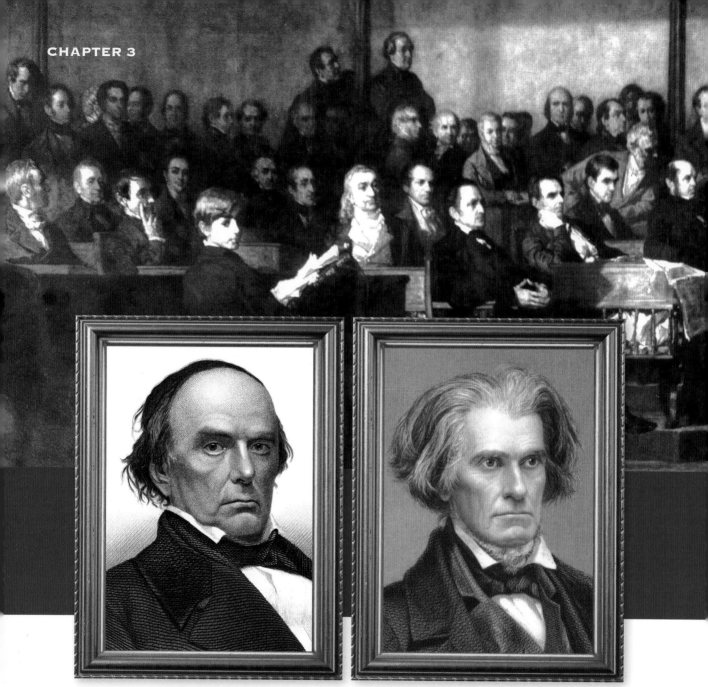

▲ Daniel Webster

▲ John Calhoun

Over the next thirty years, the nation continued to expand. More territories wanted to become states. Slavery became an issue that was slowly dividing the country.

The issue was one of human rights and **states' rights**. Should individual states have the right to accept or reject slavery? Or did the federal government have a right to decide? The Southern states were saying "no" to federal control. Southern whites wanted slavery to continue. Their crops depended on it. They did not want others telling them what to do in their states.

# Should individual states have the right to accept or reject slavery?

Speakers in the Senate presented both sides. Daniel Webster argued for the Compromise of 1850. He said, "I wish to speak today, not as a Massachusetts man, nor as a Northern man, but as an American . . . I speak today for the preservation of the Union." John Calhoun of South Carolina, on the other hand, worried that "the equilibrium [balance] between the two sections [North and South/free and slave] has been destroyed." How could the united nation continue without answering the slavery question?

## KEEPING THE BALANCE: FREE AND SLAVE

### MISSOURI COMPROMISE
Passed by Congress, 1820
Allowed Missouri to enter the Union as a slave state and Maine as a free state, thus preserving the balance of half slave and half free states. Declared no slavery in the Louisiana Purchase North of the 36° 30' latitude line, with the exception of Missouri.

### WILMOT PROVISO
Not passed, 1846
Proposed no slavery in the western lands won from Mexico; passed in the House but defeated in the Senate.

### COMPROMISE OF 1850
Passed by Congress, 1850
A series of compromises designed to avoid secession by the South, including: admission of California as a free state; New Mexico and Utah citizens allowed to vote for or against slavery; settlement of a Texas–New Mexico boundary question; a strict fugitive slave act; eliminating slave trade in the District of Columbia.

## THE FUGITIVE SLAVE ACT

On June 2, 1854, some 50,000 people lined the streets of Boston. They were shouting, booing, and crying. The president had sent Marines to keep order in the city. Out of the courthouse came nineteen-year-old Anthony Burns. Burns was a black man and he was in shackles. A troop of Marines led him from the courthouse to a ship in the harbor. The ship would carry him back to slavery in Virginia. "Kidnappers," the people of Boston screamed at the soldiers as Burns passed by.

For more than a week, the case of Anthony Burns had held the attention of everyone in Boston. A few months before, Burns had fled enslavement in Virginia. He had made his way to Boston. There, he began to build a new life as a free man. However, his owner did not intend to let him go. When the owner learned where Burns was, he went to Boston to take back his "property."

Through the Fugitive Slave Act, Anthony Burns's "owner" had the law behind him. A U.S. Marshal issued a warrant for Burns's arrest.

▲ The Fugitive Slave Act let slave owners reclaim their runaway slaves, even from Northern states.

▼ Boston was the home of many abolitionists.

## ☞HISTORICAL PERSPECTIVE

### THE FUGITIVE SLAVE ACT

The Fugitive Slave Act of 1850 increased the power of slaveholders to capture escaped slaves. Under this law, people could be held without an arrest warrant. They had no right to trial by jury. In some cases, free African Americans were captured in their own community and shipped into slavery. This law brought slavery to the North. The people in the North had to obey the law and turn in runaways. If they didn't, they faced fines and jail time. Today, we have laws that protect the rights of individuals.

▲ Published copy of the trial of Anthony Burns, 1854

Then the young man was thrown in jail. Meanwhile, word spread throughout the large abolitionist community of Boston. Led by a young minister, a group of abolitionists stormed the courthouse and tried to free Burns. Another group of African Americans mobbed the square in front of the courthouse. All efforts failed. On June 2, Burns was returned to slavery in Virginia.

The case of Anthony Burns was only one of many such events that forced Northerners to obey the laws that supported slavery. These incidents attracted people to the cause of abolitionism. More people spoke out or staged protests against slavery. More people took part in the Underground Railroad. The issue of slavery was changing from a battle into a war.

Today, we have laws that **protect the rights** of individuals.

# CHECKPOINT ☑TALK IT OVER

The Fugitive Slave Act was a law made by the U.S. government. But many people in Boston disagreed with it. Talk with a classmate about what you can do when you disagree with a law. What are some ways you can make your opinions known?

# HISTORY AND LITERATURE

### THE POWER OF UNCLE TOM'S CABIN

The Fugitive Slave Act inspired one of the greatest publishing phenomena in history: Uncle Tom's Cabin. Hating slavery, Harriet Beecher Stowe wrote the best-selling book after the Fugitive Slave Act was passed. The novel told of the horrors of slave life. It turned many people against slavery.

A famous scene in the book tells of the escape of Eliza and her child across an icy river. It was inspired by a true story. Eliza explains why she had to escape.

"I had only this [child] left . . . He was my comfort and pride, day and night; and, ma'am, they were going to take him away from me—to sell him—and sell him down South, ma'am, to go all alone—a baby that had never been away from his mother in his life! I couldn't stand it . . . when I knew the papers were signed, and he was sold, I took him and came off in the night; and they chased me . . . and I heard 'em. I jumped right on to the ice; and how I got across I don't know . . ."

▲ When it was published in 1852, *Uncle Tom's Cabin* sold 300,000 copies in the United States alone. (That would be like selling 3 million copies today!) Read around the world, the book was soon translated into thirty-seven different languages.

Eliza's dramatic ψ escape was the focus in this poster advertising a theatrical production of *Uncle Tom's Cabin*.

▲ Harriet Beecher Stowe's brother, a minister, sent arms to the abolitionists in Kansas. The guns were shipped in boxes marked "Bibles."

## "BLEEDING KANSAS"

By 1855, the United States had a preview of the violence to come. It happened in Kansas, but its effects spread across the nation. A year earlier, the Kansas–Nebraska Act had divided the Kansas Territory into two new states: Kansas and Nebraska. The act gave the people in each state the power to decide whether to be a free or a slave state. Giving power to the people through their vote is called **popular sovereignty**.

Groups of proslavery and antislavery settlers raced to the Kansas Territory to claim land. Each side was determined to win control. Soon, the groups armed themselves. In the summer of 1856, open warfare broke out between them. The violence was so bad that the state became known as "Bleeding Kansas."

One abolitionist came to stand for the violence of "Bleeding Kansas." His name was John Brown. He said that he wanted to "strike terror in the hearts of the proslavery people." He did so one May night when he killed five proslavery settlers in cold blood. But the battles over slavery were not over.

Like a fiery tornado, John Brown and his grown sons battled against those who supported slavery.

## TEXT STRUCTURE/ DESCRIPTION

Both the text and the painting describe John Brown. Words such as *like* and *as if* are clues to descriptive comparisons.

In Illinois, a young politician said of the decision, "We shall do what we can to overrule this." His name was Abraham Lincoln.

## DRED SCOTT

Some people called the Dred Scott case "the final blow." In 1857, a case related to the Fugitive Slave Act came before the U.S. Supreme Court. Dred Scott had been enslaved in Missouri. His owner brought Scott into free territory. Scott lived in the free territory for several years. Scott then claimed his freedom. The Supreme Court ruled against him.

The Court found that slaves were legally defined as property and henceforth should be treated as such. Other parts of the Court's ruling were even worse. The Chief Justice of the Court, Roger Taney, said that African Americans were not and never could be American citizens. That meant that they had no rights under the U.S. Constitution. White Southerners were happy with the ruling, while Northern abolitionists were horrified.

In Illinois, a young politician said of the decision, "We shall do what we can to overrule this." His name was Abraham Lincoln.

▲ This painting of Scott was made from a photograph in 1858. That year, white friends bought and freed Dred Scott and his wife.

## PERSONAL PERSPECTIVE

Outraged by the Dred Scott decision, author William Cullen Bryant said it made slavery "a Federal institution . . . Hereafter, wherever our . . . flag floats, it is the flag of slavery."

# SUMMING UP

- As the United States grew, so did the problem of slavery. Every new state had to be admitted to the Union as either slave or free. Each time Congress needed to make this decision, new laws were passed.

- In 1820, the Missouri Compromise formed rules that lasted for just over thirty years. The Compromise of 1850 tried to keep the balance that had been established by the earlier compromise.

- The Fugitive Slave Act further divided Northerners and Southerners over slavery.

- Events such as the trial of Anthony Burns, "Bleeding Kansas," and the Supreme Court's ruling in the Dred Scott case made the Civil War inevitable.

# PUTTING IT ALL TOGETHER

Choose one of the activities below. Work independently, in pairs, or in small groups. Share your presentation with your class.

**1** Suppose that you lived in Boston at the time of the Anthony Burns case. What would you have done? Write a letter as if you were there. Explain how you felt and what you did.

**2** Research Harriet Beecher Stowe and the publication of *Uncle Tom's Cabin*. Select a passage from the book that you think moved people either for or against slavery. Tell why the book helped the cause of the abolitionists.

**3** Reread the quote by Jefferson about the Missouri Compromise on page 25. Write a poem or create a picture or painting that conveys the fear Jefferson felt on hearing the news of the Missouri Compromise.

FIRE!

AT HARPERS FERRY

IT'S TRUE THAT I LOVE MY COUNTRY, BUT I AM A SON OF VIRGINIA.

MY FATHER WAS GOVERNOR OF THE STATE, AND A FRIEND OF GEORGE WASHINGTON, A FELLOW VIRGINIAN.

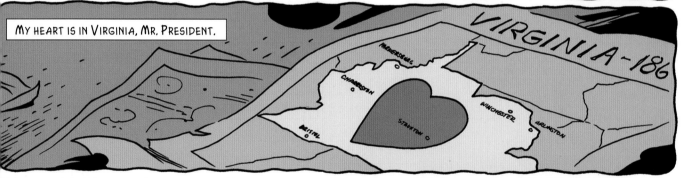

MY HEART IS IN VIRGINIA, MR. PRESIDENT.

VIRGINIA IS MY HOME.

BUT AMERICA IS YOUR COUNTRY!

WHAT SHOULD LEE DO? SHOULD HE *GHT FOR HIS HOME STATE OF VIRGINIA? OR SHOULD HE *GHT FOR THE UNION? EXPLAIN YOUR ANSWER.

# THE ROAD TO WAR IS PAVED

## What were the final events that led to the Civil War?

Abraham Lincoln is today one of the most famous names in our nation's history. In the late 1850s, however, Lincoln's name was just becoming known outside of Illinois. Lincoln had been a lawyer and had served in the Illinois legislature for six years. He had also spent two years in Congress, representing Illinois. In 1858, he ran against Stephen A. Douglas for the U.S. Senate. That race would change his life. Soon the whole nation would know Lincoln.

Lincoln and Douglas disagreed about slavery. Neither man was proslavery. Their disagreement was about how to handle both the existence and the spread of slavery. To fight Douglas on the issue, Lincoln ran against him for the Senate.

### THE LINCOLN–DOUGLAS DEBATES

The two men debated seven times. Large crowds gathered to hear them. They were on opposite sides of the slavery issue. Douglas believed that the people in each new state should decide for themselves whether to allow slavery in their state. Lincoln believed that slavery should never be allowed in new states.

"A house divided against itself cannot stand," Lincoln said. "I believe the government cannot endure [last] permanently half slave and half free." He felt that laws such as the Kansas–Nebraska Act would extend slavery rather than end it.

Douglas argued for the "sacred right of self-government." Lincoln argued for a return to the principle that "all men are created equal." Lincoln urged people to "re-adopt the Declaration of Independence."

Lincoln lost the election, but he became famous. Two years later, he was elected President of the United States.

## CHECKPOINT ✓ MAKING CONNECTIONS

Some historians consider the Lincoln–Douglas debates to be the most famous political debates in our history. How were these debates different from our debates today? How would each of these candidates have fared in today's media with our 24-hour cable news cycle? Describe what you think each would sound like speaking on television today.

> "A house divided against itself cannot stand."
>
> —Abraham Lincoln

▲ Thousands of people came to listen to the Lincoln–Douglas debates. Newspapers across the nation reported the speeches by the two men.

# CHAPTER 4

# For both sides, the ghost of John Brown would haunt the next presidential election.

### JOHN BROWN'S RAID

"Talk! Talk! Talk!" John Brown cried. "That will never free the slaves. What is needed is action—action." By 1858, Brown had turned his attention from Kansas to the South. He decided to raid a U.S. **arsenal** (a weapons storehouse) and create an army. Its goal would be to free slaves.

In October 1858, Brown led a small group against the arsenal at Harpers Ferry, Virginia. But federal troops greatly outnumbered Brown and his men. Brown was captured within thirty-six hours after the raid. He was quickly tried, convicted, and hanged.

Americans were shocked by Brown's raid. Southerners were both horrified and frightened. Many in the North, however, thought John Brown was a hero. For both sides, the ghost of John Brown would haunt the next presidential election.

▲ Paintings like this one portrayed Brown as a saint.

## 🖙 HISTORICAL PERSPECTIVE

The actions of John Brown have been controversial since he burst on the scene in Kansas. Abolitionist Frederick Douglass said Brown's zeal was like "the burning sun." Lincoln said that although he agreed with Brown "in thinking slavery wrong, that cannot excuse violence, bloodshed, and treason." Today, some people view him as a murderer, while others view him as a hero. Compare and contrast the images of John Brown on this page and page 31. How does each artist portray John Brown?

## A FATEFUL PRESIDENTIAL ELECTION

On May 18, 1860, thousands of people cheered wildly at the 1860 Republican convention in Chicago. Their "native son" from Illinois, Abraham Lincoln, had just won the nomination for president. Lincoln spent the next several months campaigning against slavery.

Southerners and other proslavery voters spoke out against Lincoln. "The Election of Lincoln is Sufficient [enough] Cause for **Secession** [leaving the Union]" was the title of a speech in Alabama. A Georgia newspaper declared, "The South will never submit to such humiliation . . . as the inauguration of Abraham Lincoln." Southern states now talked regularly about **seceding** from the Union. During the race for president, Lincoln said he hoped the South would not leave the Union. He wanted the North and South to work out the question of slavery. He wanted to keep the Union together.

Lincoln won the race for president. For Southerners, their worst fear had come true.

▲ Lincoln's running mate was Hannibal Hamlin, a U.S. senator from Maine. Hamlin became a Republican in protest against the Democrat-supported Kansas–Nebraska Act.

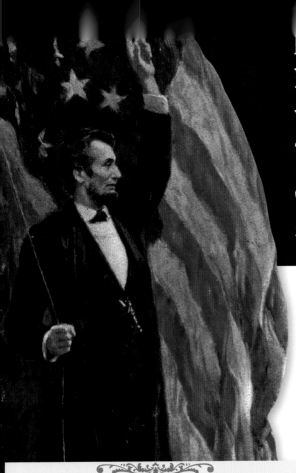

PRIMARY SOURCE

PRIMARY SOURCE
In his first inaugural speech, war was on Lincoln's mind. He said, "In your hands, my dissatisfied fellow countrymen, and not in mine, is the momentous issue of civil war."

### WAR COMES

The South's reaction was what many had feared. Southern leaders decided they could no longer be part of a nation that denied them the right to own slaves. Citing the Declaration of Independence, they said that people had the right "to alter or to abolish" the federal government. On December 20, 1860, South Carolina voted to secede. Within a few months, six other states seceded, too. Together they formed a new nation called the Confederate States of America, also called the **Confederacy**. The Union had been torn apart.

On March 4, 1861, Abraham Lincoln took the oath of office. He became the sixteenth president of the United States. He knew that war was likely.

A month later, the **Confederates** attacked Fort Sumter in South Carolina. Lincoln issued a call for troops against the Southern soldiers. The Civil War had begun.

## THE CONFEDERATE STATES OF AMERICA

| STATE | DATE OF SECESSION |
| --- | --- |
| South Carolina | December 1860 |
| Mississippi | January 1861 |
| Florida | January 1861 |
| Alabama | January 1861 |
| Georgia | January 1861 |
| Louisiana | January 1861 |
| Texas | February 1861 |
| Virginia | April 1861 |
| Arkansas | May 1861 |
| North Carolina | May 1861 |
| Tennessee | June 1861 |

[Both Kentucky and Missouri were later recognized by the Confederacy as well.]

### THE ROOT OF THE MEANING:

The words *secede* and *secession* come from the Latin verb *secedere*, meaning "to withdraw."

# SUMMING UP

- Proslavery and antislavery groups continued to battle over the issue of slavery. As the pressure of disagreement mounted, the nation moved toward a crisis.

- People across the country followed the debates in Illinois when lawyer Abraham Lincoln challenged Stephen Douglas for his Senate seat. The central issue of the campaign was slavery.

- When Lincoln won the 1860 election for president, the stage was set. The Union of states that had existed since 1776 was about to break in two.

- The break-up of the United States began when South Carolina seceded from the Union after Lincoln's election.

- By May 1861, eleven states had withdrawn from the Union. The two nations—the Confederate States of America and the United States of America—were at war.

# PUTTING IT ALL TOGETHER

Choose one of the activities below. Work independently, in pairs, or in small groups. Share your presentation with your class.

**1** Research the Lincoln–Douglas debates. Imagine that you were a newspaper reporter at the time. Write an article about one of the debates.

**2** Working with a partner, take on the roles of a Southerner and a Northerner after John Brown's raid. You might be either African American or white. Write letters to each other in which you express your reactions and opinions on Brown's actions.

**3** Create an informational map of the United States in 1861. Use the dates of secession on page 40 to label each state.

# CONCLUSION

The issues that came to a head at Fort Sumter in April 1861 had been part of America's story from the beginning. From the earliest colonies in Virginia and Massachusetts, sections of the country grew in different ways. When colonies became states, their different ways of life created conflicts. One issue continued to challenge the Union. That issue was slavery.

At first, Americans worked hard to find compromises between the proslavery and antislavery groups. But over time, the compromises no longer worked. The battles over slavery became violent. Finally, the nation broke into civil war.

**1607: Jamestown is settled in what will one day be known as the state of Virginia.**

**1776: Declaration of Independence states "All men are created equal . . ." yet enslaved African Americans were not treated as equal and were not free.**

**1793: Invention of the cotton gin increases demand for cotton and slave labor in the South.**

**1800: Immigrants begin entering the North.**

**1820: Missouri Compromise evens out number of slave and free states.**

**1600**    **1700**    **1800**    **1825**

**1787: The creation of the U.S. Constitution reflects the conflict over states' rights and slavery.**

**1810–1850: At its height, the Underground Railroad helps an estimated 30,000–100,000 enslaved African Americans escape to freedom.**

# Today, war can still divide people. However, since the Civil War, the United States has remained one nation.

It was a war that many on both sides tried to avoid. In the end, however, Abraham Lincoln refused to allow the Union to dissolve. He believed that war was necessary to "maintain the . . . existence of our National Union."

Today, war can still divide people. However, since the Civil War, the United States has remained one nation. The federal government works to solve problems and resolve issues that exist between regions to keep the Union strong.

**1857:** The Dred Scott ruling is overturned by the Supreme Court.

**1831:** Nat Turner Rebellion

**1852:** *Uncle Tom's Cabin* is published and sells 300,000 copies.

**1854:** Fugitive Slave Law is passed.

**1858:** John Brown's Raid

**1861:** First shots fired on Fort Sumter on April 12.

## 1830    1840    1850    1860

**1856:** "Bleeding Kansas"

**1860:** Lincoln is elected president.

South Carolina secedes from the Union and is soon followed by other Southern states.

**1838: Anti-Slavery Convention of American Women is held in Philadelphia.**

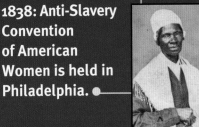

# HOW TO WRITE A LETTER TO THE EDITOR

On March 8, 1857, articles in the *Cincinnati Enquirer* praised the Supreme Court's decision in the Dred Scott case. But articles in the *New York Tribune* and the *Chicago Tribune* said it was a terrible decision. Just as happens today, newspapers in the 1800s took different stands on important political issues of the day.

For as long as there have been newspapers in this country, Americans have been writing letters to their editors. In the days before television interviews and the Internet, letters to the editor (sometimes called LTEs) were an important way for readers to share their ideas. They still are today.

Newspapers receive many more letters than they can print. Take a look at the LTEs in one or more papers. Think about why the editors chose to print those letters.

## How-To . . .

### Plan Your Letter

1. **Choose an issue that would have been in the news in the years leading up to the Civil War. The issue should be one on which people had strong and differing opinions.**
2. **Read more about the issue. Decide what your opinion is.**
3. **Research quotes, statistics, and other information to support your opinion.**
4. **Outline the points that you wish to make in a letter of several paragraphs. (Note the length of LTEs in the newspapers you read.)**

### Write Your Letter

1. **In the first paragraph, clearly state the issue and your opinion in a few sentences.**
2. **Make each point in a short paragraph. Include facts and quote experts when appropriate.**
3. **Keep your tone informative rather than emotional. Keep your letter short and make your points clearly.**
4. **In your final paragraph, summarize your opinion and thank the editor.**

# SAMPLE: AN OPINION LETTER TO THE EDITOR

Dear Editor:

In the March 8 edition of your newspaper, you supported Chief Justice Taney's Supreme Court decision in Dred Scott v. Sandford. I strongly disagree with Chief Justice Taney's arguments and with the Cincinnati Enquirer's position.

Two issues are at the heart of Taney's opinion. The first is the question of citizenship. Justice Taney states that Dred Scott is not a citizen. He says that Negroes were never citizens and were not to share in the rights listed in the Constitution. I disagree with Justice Taney. The Declaration of Independence states a truth that I believe in. It says that "all men are created equal." This means everyone, in my opinion. Therefore, Dred Scott and all black Americans should be citizens.

The second issue involves property. Justice Taney says that an enslaved person is property, not a person. I believe that no human being can be considered property. About 4 million human beings are enslaved in America. They are human beings, not property.

I believe that the Supreme Court made a grave mistake in the Dred Scott case. This decision will only lead to greater conflict. I fear for our nation.

Thank you for your attention.

Sincerely,
Jane Smith

Don't forget to thank the editor!

# GLOSSARY

**abolitionist**  (a-buh-LIH-shun-ist) *noun* a person who wanted to abolish, or end, slavery (page 20)

**antebellum**  (an-tih-BEH-lum) *adjective* belonging to the period before the Civil War (page 15)

**arsenal**  (AR-seh-nul) *noun* a place where the government stores weapons and ammunition (page 38)

**Confederacy**  (kun-FEH-duh-ruh-see) *noun* the eleven Southern states that declared themselves separate from the United States in 1860 and 1861 (page 40)

**Confederate**  (kun-FEH-duh-rut) *noun* a person who fought for or supported the Confederacy (page 40)

**emancipate**  (ih-MAN-sih-pate) *verb* to free, specifically to free from slavery (page 20)

**free state**  (FREE STATE) *noun* a state in which slavery was illegal (page 12)

**fugitive**  (FYOO-jih-tiv) *noun* a person who runs away or tries to escape (page 20)

**immigrant**  (IH-mih-grunt) *noun* a person who moves to a country from another place (page 7)

**Industrial Revolution**  (in-DUS-tree-ul reh-vuh-LOO-shun) *noun* the rapid change in the economy that occurred in the late eighteenth century, driven by the invention and use of new high-powered machines (page 6)

| | |
|---|---|
| mill | (MIL) *noun* building in which machinery is used to process raw materials into finished products (page 7) |
| pioneer | (py-uh-NEER) *noun* a person who is one of the first to do something or go somewhere (page 12) |
| plantation | (plan-TAY-shun) *noun* a large farm on which crops are raised (page 10) |
| popular sovereignty | (PAH-pyuh-ler SAH-vuh-ren-tee) *noun* a system in which residents vote to decide an issue (page 31) |
| rural | (RER-ul) *adjective* in the country (page 11) |
| secede | (sih-SEED) *verb* to formally withdraw from membership in an organization, alliance, or nation (page 39) |
| secession | (sih-SEH-shun) *noun* the act of seceding (page 39) |
| slave state | (SLAVE STATE) *noun* a state in which slavery was legal (page 12) |
| slavery | (SLAY-vuh-ree) *noun* the condition in which one person has complete control or "ownership" over another (page 10) |
| states' rights | (STATES RITES) *noun* the political belief that limits the power of the federal government and reserves rights to the states (page 26) |
| Underground Railroad | (un-der-GROWND RALE-rode) *noun* the network that aided people escaping from slavery before the Civil War (page 19) |

# INDEX